Other Works by John J. Errigo, M.S.:

A Lean Marketing Revolution:
The Timeless Know-How Principles
(Summer, 2011)

Level UP: Lead with Emotional Intelligence
(Fall, 2011)

The Big Bang Entrepreneur:
When Start Ups and Ethics Collide
(Winter, 2012)

Public Domain Works with Introductions and arrangements by John J. Errigo, M.S.:

The Science of Getting Rich (Wattles)
(Winter, 2012)

The Laws of Success in Sixteen Lessons (Hill)
(Winter, 2012)

The Art of War: Chopped (Sun-tzu)
(Spring, 2012)

Published by Quincentennial Publishing Company

Published in the United States of America

Cover Art designed by Award Winning Graphic Artist
Eric Zempol: http://www.eric-z.com

eISBN (13) 978-0-9849828-8-2
Print ISBN: 978-1-940927-14-5

Any questions or comments please write to the author at:
john@johnerrigo.com

Green Oak Press
Print Edition
Spring 2014

Quotes

"If a member is willing to stay on a team when offered a chance to leave,
this is seen as a member who belongs to a cohesive team."
(Shaw, 1976)

If you must slander someone don't speak it- but write it –
write it in the sand, near the water's edge!
(Napoleon Hill)

TIME is a Master Worker that heals the wounds of temporary defeat,
and equalizes the inequalities and rights the wrongs of the world.
There is nothing "Impossible" with time!
(Unknown)

No man has a chance to enjoy permanent success
until he begins to look in the mirror
for the real cause of all his mistakes.
(Napoleon Hill)

Don't always have the last word; sometimes you
just have to be quiet to get along with others.
(Marie Taylor)

Dedication

To my grandmother, Marie Lucas Taylor,
a beautiful woman who taught me so much
about getting along with others.
She taught me how to remain calm, cool, collected,
and hold-up well with class in times of adversity.

Special Thanks To

My mom who spends her lunch and some free time,
making sure my work is understandable.

Alejandro who is translating my EI works to Spanish:
your dedication and support are simply the best.

Gerry Mayers who dedicates special attention
to each detail in this and every booklet.

Nina for her willingness to help, her skills,
and her gracious advice.

Eric Zempol for his
awesome covers and ideas.

Kais for knowing how to pick out
the best chocolate in Canada!

MAKING TEAMS "STICK" TOGETHER

Emotional Intelligence and Team Cohesion

BY JOHN ERRIGO, MS
EDITED BY GERARD E. MAYERS

Contents

Preface

Have you ever wanted to work in, or be part of, a great team? All of us have worked in teams in a variety of formats throughout our lives. Most of us have either enjoyed the experience or found it anything but perfect. This booklet will help define what a good team is, how to make it stick, and how the emotionally intelligent leader puts together good and cohesive teams. Finally, this booklet also will help you learn what good team leaders are, how to spot them, and how to become part of a great team.

The What, Why, Where, and How of Cohesion

At a recent training seminar, a participant asked me: "What do you mean by 'cohesion'?" As someone who earned his Master's degree investigating the areas of leadership, emotional intelligence, and team cohesion, I thought it was a word everyone knew. To my great dismay, I did not have a 30-second elevator speech for this person; I was a bit embarrassed. If I could re-do the scenario, I would try to say something like this: "Cohesion is the simple act of people who want to stay within a team, company, unit, business partner, etc., if they had the chance to move to another venue." This was not the definition you were thinking? Right? Well, neither was I until I came across a study by two researchers in the late 1980s from The Netherlands. This was their simple answer: Cohesion is wishing to remain in a group when there is a chance to move to another.

Think about this concept for a minute. If you had the chance in your current job, to move to a different job, regardless of location and work somewhere else, would you go? If the answer is yes, then you are not working in a cohesive manner. I will go a step further: This same rule can apply to relationships, friendships, teammates, business partners, and companies.

Cohesion is the fabric of society and the manner in which we find contentment. We either have cohesive relationships or we do not. We either have cohesive families or we do not. We either work in a cohesive team or we do not. The focus of this booklet is a novel one since there is not a lot written about the true nature of team cohesion and emotional intelligence. While preparing my Master's thesis, I had to build the bridges of scholarly research between emotional intelligence and team cohesion. There was scant literature on the topic. It is my pleasure to now present to you a guidebook on cohesive teams (how to develop and recognize them) and building them with emotional intelligence to improve their efficacy.

Leadership is the Glue in Cohesive Team Development

It would be tremendous if all bosses knew how to put together good teams. The fact is they do not. Why? It is probably due to a whole range of reasons. The main one might simply be because your boss either is limited in his or her power to have the people he or she would like to work together, or simply has no clue on how to build a cohesive team, or is simply not sure who would work well together. A mix or all of the above would probably suffice here.

Good leaders, i.e., those with emotional intelligence, know who will work well together. It takes extraordinary leaders to put together a good team. They know who will work together, not just by trial and error, but by knowing the intimate details of each person's character, personality, and how they will gel with others. (This is a sure sign of an emotionally intelligent leader.) The next time you have a talk with your boss, if your boss is in the extraordinary column, he or she is probably sizing you up to see who you would work best with. He or she is probably doing this with all of your teammates. If you have a "disaster" boss (which most of us have had in our lives), then this person is clueless and will never be able to put together a good evaluation of your job performance, let alone a cohesive team.

It is good leadership which drives the formation of teams. It should not be happenstance when forming a team, and it should definitely not be by trial and error. But, if it has to be that way, it should not be a frequent occurrence. We all know when a leader puts together a team by mere happenstance. People do not readily get along; some people are not committed to the task at hand; and even more telling, people are ready to jump ship when the next opportunity or promotion arrives, just to be off the team. We have all been there. Some of us have even been in the room when a leader is trying to pick the team members, and you thought to yourself, "This is not going to work." Oftentimes it does not. Let's examine what happens when a leader makes the right choices and *why*.

A leader who has a good sense of emotional intelligence would be best able to put together a good team.

Although not perfect, this emotionally intelligent leader is automatically in the "extraordinary boss" column. There are plenty of emotionally intelligent leaders who are not perfect and not God-sent. In an article appearing a few years ago in *Time* Magazine, noted emotional intelligence expert Daniel Goleman commented that emotional intelligence is not the only predictor of success. While he did not use these exact words, he mentioned emotional intelligence basically has the ability to push a person's job performance from the mediocre column to the good column, but it also takes cognitive abilities *and* emotional intelligence to be on the path to greatness. I would also add, this comment would be best suited for those in executive roles.

I would argue wholeheartedly that, if all the circumstances fell into place (such as budgeting, hiring the right staff, ability to motivate people, building and motivating cross-departmental work groups, etc.), emotionally intelligent leaders would put together better teams.

People who do not have emotional intelligence under control, or have no clue of the concept, might also put together pretty good teams. I would, however, bet they are not cohesive, which I propose is the ultimate argument in professional life (especially in the gritty areas of the work environment).

Imagine working with people who are not only as good as you, but perhaps have an ability to bring out the best in you, and stretch your abilities and creativity. These are the people who make life easy for you and enjoyable, and you only experience it when working in a cohesive manner.

Emotionally intelligent leaders would be best at putting together good teams. They know people quite well, since through their observation, self-reflection, and dealings with others, they attract the best people, and people want to work with them. Also, through their careful observation and dealings with others, they get to know how people "tick" and the personalities of others, and are able to imagine who would work well together. These traits are what make the emotionally intelligent leader good at putting together cohesive teams.

Emotionally Intelligent Leaders: Great Motivators to Develop

To develop a cohesive team, a leader must first develop the foundational elements of his or her staff. These foundational elements include the relationship between the leader and staff, understanding those areas of growth which need to be targeted, what motivates each member of the team to produce his/her best work, etc. Emotionally intelligent leaders will always aim to understand where their staff are coming from and then how to proceed in developing them. They will know what areas they need to act and how to act accordingly:

> "Leaders must know how to act, as well as when to act based on characteristics of self, others (followers) and situations (environments) within which they lead. Understanding one's emotions and developing the wisdom to apply that knowledge is critical to the appropriate application of emotional intelligence."[1]

A leader who knows how to act and when will be more effective in achieving the desired outcomes. The leader's emotional intelligence will be a compass for the developmental needs of his/her staff.

Another useful theory in understanding emotional intelligence, sometimes known as EI or EQ, (I prefer EI as shorthand for Emotional Intelligence) and how it relates to staff development is an Emotional Quotient Matrix, which is based upon the tenets of emotional intelligence. The dimensions of the matrix are emotional strengths verses weaknesses and controllable versus uncontrollable traits. According to Service and Fekula, emotional intelligence is a leadership imperative and emotion plays a significant role in leadership. The researchers also believe strongly that emotion and leadership (human influence) together "make for an outstanding partnership since leaders then are able to influence a variety of situations based upon the knowledge they gain from observing others."[2] Leadership and EI *do* go hand-in-hand.

Service and Fekula also state: "EI/EQ is the sum total of the leadership's ability to know and use one's emotions, as well as read and use the emotions of others. It amounts to emotional maturity and is comprised of a range of traits including energy level, stress tolerance, confidence, locus of control and emotional and social stability."[3] Leaders who manage their emotions and read the emotions of others are better able to lead their followers in the workplace since they can gauge a situation and know how to influence their staff to action. Without it, they can not succeed.[4] Leaders who are able to motivate their staff and influence them to action are successful in leading them in accomplishing organizational objectives. Rosete and Ciarrochi state: "Leaders who use the components of EI, namely idealized influence, inspirational motivation and individual consideration, were assumed to be more effective in the workplace."[5]

Positive leadership has been associated with outcomes that include happy relationships, teamwork, learning, recognition, and staff retention. These are positive characteristics since a leader is able to recognize when these positive characteristics are important, when to employ them and use them to bring people and projects together. These same positive characteristics are paramount when putting together a cohesive team and emotional intelligence brings about this awareness in a leader.

In order to develop their staff, leaders need to positively influence them in order to facilitate behavioral changes which will contribute to their overall professional development. These competencies are also instrumental in developing teams and working with a collective staff to accomplish larger organizational objectives, i.e., building effective and cohesive teams.

Leadership generally consists of such dimensions as having a vision, power, utilization, delegation, discipline, supervision, and external monitoring.[6] According to Blattner and Bacigalupo, a "team" implies a group of people who pull together in a strong, cohesive and complementary fashion to support the leader's vision and aspirations.[7] It is the function of the team to carry out the mission of the leader (by who it is influenced) and it is the leader who sets the tone and develops the team. The leader has a tremendous influence on the emotions of the team and how the team sees itself. It is emotionally intelligent leaders who provide the drive for individual members to perform as part of their teams.[8] "The leader's overall charisma, motivational influence, intellectual stimulation, and individualized attention to team members create [sic] an atmosphere of empowerment."[9]

The leader also influences the team's behavior. If a leader makes each team member feel important and fosters the growth of each individual team member, then the leader will create an effective and cohesive team. The leader has to have the emotional intelligence necessary to be able to identify where and how to foster growth of each team member. This happens with observing others and having an awareness of others and their subsequential motivations. One researcher correctly reasoned that the emotionally intelligent leader can accurately assess others' emotions and constructively influence those emotions: "The leader needs to know exactly when and how to access and subsequently influence the emotions of the individual team members to achieve a collective goal or objective."[10]

Emotion, therefore, becomes a key component in any leader's ability to create charismatic authority over the members of the team to ensure team transformation. During the American Civil War of 1861-1865, it was the responsibility of the commanding officer of each regiment North or South, to insure his men were properly drilled as well as clothed and fed. Each regimental commander was answerable to his higher authority for any derelictions. In the beginning, the soldiers grumbled and complained mightily about the incessant drill imposed upon them. This, however, changed drastically once combat was joined. Because he was such a stickler for drilling and proper procedures, Robert McAllister of the Eleventh Regiment, New Jersey Volunteer Infantry, originally was spoken of derisively as "Mother McAllister." After the regiment's horrendous firefight at the Klingle farm on July 2, 1863 at Gettysburg, surviving members looked upon their colonel with affection and high respect. Previously used in derision, "Mother McAllister" now became a term showing the regiment's transformation. By all the definitions cited above, McAllister had fashioned a cohesive and an effective team.[11]

The degree to which a leader is able to arouse, inspire and motivate individuals is closely related to the level of emotional intelligence possessed by that leader.[12] The leader has to know when to regulate emotions for the common good of the team and when to use them effectively for a given purpose. The emotional intelligence of the leader is closely tied to the ability to influence others; this influence helps nurture and guides each individual team member.

To use an example, a team leader seeks to influence his team members about a new training program. A leader who promotes training uses a careful display of emotions. The leader's enthusiasm for the program helps create an atmosphere of excitement by being positive and upbeat in explaining the benefits of such training. An emotionally aware leader will know exactly how to display the necessary emotions (enthusiasm, excitement, positive language, willingness to take the training as well) to effectively inspire team members. As a result, the leader's influence over the team as well as its reactions and emotions has a tremendous impact on cohesive team development.

In the article *Group Development and Team Effectiveness,* Bushe and Coetzer contend there are different stages of group development. The primary stage is group membership, where the leader has a great impact on the developing team. "The first phase of development in teams is membership. It is [considered] the first phase because until members psychologically join, there is not [a] team but just a collection of individuals who have been grouped together."[13] The collection of individuals exists first; it is the function of the leader to bring them together and develop them into a cohesive team. These two researchers believe strongly that for a team to successfully develop, "its members must want to belong to the team and come to identify with the team."[14] The leader is the one who has to work with each individual team member to help them identify with the team. The leader puts forth the effort to collectively identify with each member, where the team members will benefit by collectively identifying with each other.

Perhaps a member is placed in a team in order to foster professional growth and development as well as to achieve organizational objectives. Since the emotionally intelligent team leader is aware of the professional growth needs of each team member and how to nurture this growth, he or she can make the proper decisions based on reading the emotional responses observed. "Emotions can provide leaders with information about problems and opportunities and leaders can determine when emotions are linked to opportunities, problems or proposed courses of action, and use those emotions as information in the process of making decisions."[15] Once a leader has identified which people would be best suited to work together, the team identity will be formed as a result of the psychologically joined members who will recognize a synergistic dynamic among each other. *Teams are increasingly becoming the foundation of where organizational objectives are being implemented and met.* It is the emotionally intelligent leader who will successfully develop cohesive teams to meet these objectives.

Leaders Who Excel and Hit the Ball
Out of the Park!

"Over the last decade, virtually all organizations, from production to commercial retailing to customer service firms, have begun utilizing the work team structure to some degree within their operations."[16] The team and its development are critically important for the effective realization of company objectives and outcomes. It takes good leadership to develop a solid team. "Leadership is generally accepted as those behaviors that influence a group's ability to set goals and complete tasks."[17]

Emotionally intelligent leaders will be able to understand closely the individual traits and behaviors of their employees and make adjustments to their own behaviors and attitudes to be more effective when working with their staff.[18] This statement alone will help a leader develop a stellar team and hit the ball out of the park with performance. As mentioned previously (see the booklet *Level Up: Lead with Emotional Intelligence*), people who are emotionally intelligent possess a keen sense of self-awareness as well as an awareness of others.

Emotionally aware leaders can adjust their behavior to the environment and the individual traits of their employees. Thamhain's research (2004) demonstrates that the working environment within the project team has a significant impact on project success and therefore suggests that the "project manager has a significant leadership role in fusing the team."[19] *The leader alone is responsible for forming the team and providing the context in how other team members will behave with each other.* The way the leader interacts with the team will set an example of how the team members will interact with each other and will foster an environment that is mutually beneficial. A perfect example of this in a fictional context would be the CBS show *NCIS* wherein Special Agent Leroy Jethro Gibbs has carefully put together a very cohesive and dynamic (as well as successful) team of investigators.

Kloppenborg and Petrick suggest "project leaders have a role in developing team characteristics into a collective set of virtues including: ethics, respect and trust for others, honesty, prudence, courage, responsible use and sharing power."[20] A leader's emotional intelligence will foster these team characteristics because the leader will know how these characteristics operate within individual team members. As a result of the leader's developing team characteristics, he will be able to achieve team cohesion. Because "individuals will see themselves and be seen by others as members of a group who are interdependent because of the tasks they perform as members of a group," it is the team leader who has the heaviest responsibility of fostering team cohesion.[21]

It is the leader who creates (and influences) the environment for team members who want to be motivated to remain. The quality of these interpersonal relationships within the team and their development are shaped largely by the team leader himself/herself. As a result, members are motivated to remain on the team where the quality of these relationships are well developed. Cohesion indicates the degree to which members of a team are motivated to remain on the team. If a member is willing to stay on a team when offered a chance to leave, this is seen as a member who belongs to a cohesive team.[22]

Feyerherm and Rice analyzed leaders' emotional intelligence and the correlation of team performance. In their study, they found "emotional intelligence is not a panacea to performance; however, emotional intelligence is important to developing team dynamics."[23] It is the team leader's interactions with individual members which strengthens the team structure. "A work team's success on a project depends to a large degree on effective interactions among [the] team members responsible for the project."[24] An emotionally intelligent leader will foster these effective interactions with the individual members of the team and will build the structure of the developing team through these effective relationships.

> "As a developing team, there will
> be a mixture of collective emotions
> that a leader must carefully manage.
> Emotionally intelligent leaders will be
> aware of these emotions in their staff
> and how to appropriately handle

them. Emotions and behaviors
experienced and or encountered by
managers and their staff may include
fear and anxiety, insecurity, defensive
or irrational behavior, anger,
aggression, arrogance and controlling
behavior."[25]

In order to develop a cohesive team, it is important that a leader recognizes these negative emotions and understands where they are coming from. The emotionally intelligent leader will work through these negative emotions, which will help further develop the team. Once the negative emotions are worked through, the positive emotions of a team may surface. The emotionally intelligent leader will work towards developing the positive qualities of each team member first, in order to facilitate development of a positive collective identity that will be formed as a result.

"Individual consideration is directed at treating followers as individuals and not just members of a group."[26] *It is important that the leader develops the potential of each individual, not just the collective potential encompassed by the members of the team.* Behaviors related to individualized consideration include a leader who spends time in teaching and coaching, helping others develop their strengths and listening attentively to others' concerns; this behavior strengthens subordinates' confidence and molds them.[27]

An emotionally intelligent leader can coach a team member in areas needed for professional growth, based upon careful observation of behaviors. Effective interactions between the team leader and the individual members will help increase the members' ability to function more effectively. The EI of a leader will help mold the interactions of the team and the collective team as a whole since the leader will know what areas of communication and/or behaviors need to be targeted. "After all, effective team functioning is contingent, at least in part, on individuals mentally processing affective information and using it to engage in effective interactions with fellow team members."[28] It is the leader who fosters effective interactions with fellow team members, since this will allow them to know *when* and *how* to act.

In a study presented recently, Jennifer George found there is a very significant link between emotionally intelligent leaders and the development of high quality interpersonal relationships.[29] George discovered this link has lead to increased leadership effectiveness when developing individuals and teams in general. "Leaders who are high on emotional intelligence may instill in their organizations a sense of enthusiasm, excitement, and optimism as well as an atmosphere of cooperation and trust through their being able to develop high quality interpersonal relationships with their followers."[30] These high quality interpersonal relationships are instrumental when building a cohesive team, since an emotionally intelligent leader is able to influence and promote action based upon the relationships formed.

Leaders who are aware and sensitive to the particular needs of their subordinates can read the social requirements of situations. They know what to do to enlist, direct, and facilitate the dedication of individual effort and team performance; this observation of others and the appropriate response and/or action is a skill that is closely linked to emotional intelligence.[31] The EI of a leader will help facilitate the development of a cohesive team since he/she will know when to act, and what needs to be done to improve team functioning which happens at both the individual and collective level.

One way to help develop individuals and team performance, according to Goleman, is through the various competencies related to EI.[32] This is the "ability to recognize and understand emotions and the skill to use this awareness to manage self and the relationships with others."[33] The emotionally intelligent leader will be able to manage his own emotions, be aware of others' emotions, and be more effective in dealing with each individual team member as a result.

"Empathy, another component of emotional intelligence, was associated with team viability through team cohesion."[34] Empathetic behavior modeled by an emotionally intelligent leader increases team morale since the leader knows the team members' motivations and emotions. The establishment of empathetic behavior as a team norm will cause relationships to be built and a strong social support network of the team to be formed.[35]

The relational dimension of the team is important to team cohesion. The emotionally intelligent leader will be able to manage the emotions of team members (which will help the team work towards a collective objective, the formation of a cohesive team).

"Emotional intelligence is associated in several important ways within interpersonal relationships. Qualities expected to facilitate more successful relationships (e.g., empathic perspective taking, self-monitoring, good social skills, cooperation) were related to emotional intelligence."[36] Emotionally intelligent leaders will know how to foster the healthy dynamics of interpersonal relationships with their staff which will assist in developing a successful and cohesive team.

"Cohesiveness is an important characteristic of teams, because team members are more willing to show cooperative behavior to each other."[37] When developing a cohesive team, an emotionally intelligent leader must strive to manage the behaviors and emotional states of their team members. "Leadership is intrinsically an emotional process, whereby leaders recognize followers' emotional states, attempt to evoke emotions in followers, and then seek to manage followers' emotional states accordingly."[38]

Emotionally intelligent leadership might enable a leader to be better able to monitor how work group members are feeling, and take the appropriate action.[39] If an emotionally intelligent leader recognizes the group is struggling emotionally, perhaps as a result of a conflict, the leader will be able to mediate and take appropriate action based upon his assessment of the situation.

The emotionally intelligent leader is able to take appropriate action since he or she knows the group well as well as the central foundations of communication and the emotional well being of the group. The emotional intelligence of a leader then is central to the development of a cohesive team. The success of the relationships built in the cohesive team is a result of emotionally intelligent leadership. "Leaders are responsible for the success of the teams they lead."[40] Because of this, according to Rafaeli and Worline, leaders are also responsible for the emotions of the teams they lead, in addition to their own.[41]

An "Aha!" Moment –

Salovey and Mayer described emotional intelligence as being able to closely watch one's own feelings and emotions as well as those of others, to distinguish between them and then use the intelligence thus gathered to guide one's own thinking and actions.[42] This basic definition of the emotional intelligence theory has set the stage for further discussion on the impacts of EI on workplace performance, interpersonal effectiveness, leadership, and a leader's development of cohesive teams. Research has demonstrated emotional intelligence is a developing theory, which is instrumental in the workplace as well as within leadership effectiveness.

These three sentences are the "Aha!" moment: 1. EI allows leaders to pick up the subtle nuances of emotions and to apply those emotions to effectively manage the staff they lead. 2. A leader's emotional awareness as well as that of others go a long way towards effective staff development. 3. Based on careful observation of others, an effective leader knows when and how to act as well as how to properly influence staff to achieve organizational objectives and goals.

Key to proper building of a cohesive team is establishing effective interpersonal relationships with each member of the team and then with the team as a whole. A truly emotionally intelligent leader is able to recognize the steps needed to do this, act on the information gathered, build the relationships and forge a cohesive team in the process. Part of building an effective interpersonal relationship with each team member is knowing what each member can bring to the team and what motivates each member to want to be part of the team. Because effective leaders can make the proper decisions to achieve desired outcomes, they can foster the development and growth of cohesive teams. Emotionally intelligent leaders build teams because they manage their emotions and the emotions of others to develop a collective identity.

The True Synergy in Making Teams "Stick" Together

As with most things in life and in work, nothing is perfect. We do have a choice however, in all of the areas of our life. One choice is to be part of a team which can stick together, through thick and thin. While we may look to the leader to make this happen, we are just as responsible to make it work too. For many years, I was more than happy to play the "blame game," and make all of my bad working relationships a result of someone else's behavior or actions. I never once looked at my own actions that contributed to these relationships and the way they eventually panned out.

It is easy then to always put the blame on the leader, and say, "Well, my boss is responsible for the results and the way the team turned out!" While twenty percent of this statement is true, the other eighty percent has a lot to do with our actions, behaviors, and how we contribute to the team. My recommendation is: If you are put together in a team, and you are not sure you can stick together, at least give it your best effort. In doing so, you might be pleasantly surprised at how well things work out.

Like any good relationship, it gets better each and every day, and it takes work. Nothing magical can happen unless you put in the work. The same is true for being on a good team. The boss has the responsibility to lay the foundation by picking the right people to work together, and to nurture the team. The rest is up to us.

A parting thought: We make the choice ultimately to stick together in a team. With the right ingredients, and the right mix of leadership and emotional intelligence, we can rise to the occasion. We can do this by making a decision to stick together rather than pointing the stick.

The Quick Nitty Gritty of Q & A
(EI and Teams)

Some questions are proper here to understanding the impact of effective leadership, emotional intelligence, and interpersonal relationships on building cohesive teams.

Table 1.0: Frequency of Team Leader and Encouraging Team Members' Professional Growth

"My team leader is supportive of my professional growth."

Answers	Frequency	Percent	Valid Percent	Cumulative Percent
Agree	7	41.2	41.2	41.2
Somewhat agree	6	35.3	35.3	76.5
Neither agree/disagree	2	11.8	11.8	88.2
Somewhat disagree	2	11.8	11.8	100.0
Total	17	100.0	100.0	

Does the emotional intelligence of a leader have a positive impact on the development of cohesive teams?

Yes. Research seems to indicate, at this point, that the emotional intelligence of a leader *does* have a positive impact on the development of cohesive teams. In the research study, when asked if a team member would leave their current team and join another, only 5.9% of the respondents said, "Yes." 76.4% disagreed or somewhat disagreed. 17.6% neither agreed nor disagreed. These high numbers indicate team cohesion. As defined by Shaw earlier in this booklet, the cohesion of a team is defined as the degree to which a team member would prefer to remain on the team rather than leave.

The high response rate about leaders who possess emotional intelligence would suggest their leadership positively impacts on the development of cohesive teams. The frequency tabulation incorporating all teams from the above table reveals 41% agree, 35.3% somewhat agree, and 11.8% somewhat disagree. This is a pretty high number of statistical information that helps define the leader as having a considerable impact on the support system of the individual team members.

Based upon these statistics, it has been found the leader does have a positive impact on the development of cohesive teams.

Table 1.1: Frequency of Team Leader's Helpfulness to Team Member

"My team leader is helpful to me."			
Answers	Frequency	Percent	Valid Percent	Cumulative Percent
Agree	8	47.1	47.1	47.1
Somewhat agree	7	41.2	41.2	88.2
Neither agree/disagree	2	11.8	11.8	100.0
Total	17	100.0	100.0	

Does the emotional intelligence of a leader have a positive impact on the developmental needs of a forming team?

Yes. Based upon the statistical analysis of the data, the leader's emotional intelligence does impact on the developmental needs of a forming team. The frequency data of all the teams combined would suggest the teams' leaders were helpful to all the team members. 47.1% of the respondents agreed their team leader was helpful to them; 41.2% of the respondents agreed their team leader was somewhat helpful to them. Only 11.8% could not agree or disagree their team leader was helpful to them. According to this data, the emotionally intelligent leaders were helpful to the team members. This would also suggest it had something to do with each team's developmental needs and the subsequent cohesiveness of the team.

When the question was asked about the leader's importance of working on the developmental needs of others, there was total agreement (100%) among all the team members. This would also suggest they have a role in the developmental needs of the individual team members.

Based upon the data above, it would appear that an emotionally intelligent leader has a tremendous impact on the developmental needs of the forming team.

Summary of Findings in Research/Conclusions

A s noted previously, the research and the data suggest all teams were cohesive as well as all leaders were emotionally intelligent. This is truly insightful since a leader's emotional intelligence or EI has an impact on developing cohesive teams. The emotionally intelligent leader was supportive to the developmental needs of the team members, as well as the emotional needs of each team member, which resulted in a cohesive team.

It has been proven that the emotionally intelligent leader knows exactly when and how to access and subsequently influence the emotions of the individual team members to achieve a collective goal or objective: "Therefore, one who is emotionally intelligent might use emotion to create charismatic authority over team members in order to ensure team transformation."[43]

All the leaders (100%) surveyed felt it was important to work on the developmental needs of the team members. Of the team members themselves, 41% agree, 35.3% somewhat agree, and 11.8% somewhat disagree that the team leader is supportive to the professional growth of individual team members. The emotionally intelligent leader is aware of their emotions and the emotions of others.

The researcher who did the study discovered that, out of all the leaders, 66.7% agree and 33.3% somewhat agree that they correctly interpret the emotions of the team members. All the leaders surveyed agreed it was important to know when to use these emotions and regulate them for the collective purposes of developing a cohesive team.[44] The leader has to know when to regulate those emotions for the common good of the team and use them effectively for a given purpose. The degree of emotional intelligence of a leader is closely connected to an ability and an efficiency in that ability to arouse, inspire and lead individuals.[45] A leader's emotional intelligence is very closely tied to an ability to influence others; this influence helps nurture and guide each individual team member. A leader's emotional intelligence has a direct impact on the successful development of a cohesive team.

There Are Limitations in Proven
Realities like Team Development

There were limitations on the study. The survey used to measure a leader's emotional intelligence was not a valid or reliable instrument even though it had been tested in prior research. The survey questions came from a study done by Daniel Goleman, a noted researcher on emotional intelligence. Goleman divided emotional intelligence into four major subsections: self-management, self-awareness, social awareness and relationship management. The researcher took questions from each sub-section and developed the instrument in the study to analyze emotional intelligence.

The other limitation was the sample size. The study consisted of seventeen subjects (from three teams); the data would have been much richer and perhaps more insightful (and the hypothesis tested on a larger scale) if a larger sampling group was available. Although the study proved the hypothesis adequately, it would have been interesting (for example) if there were ten teams and ten team leaders to survey. More data would have been collected and the underlying hypothesis that emotionally intelligent leaders make effective team coaches and build cohesive teams would have readily been tested on a much larger scale.

Errigo's Emotional Intelligence Survey

This survey is adapted from Daniel Goleman's tool in determining Emotional Intelligence based on his four identified quadrants of EI, along with additional questions developed from John Errigo's own research. Errigo also used this survey as a method in his Master's Thesis to determine EI in leadership.

Instructions: Write down on a piece of paper 1 to 16. Answer each question as you read it; write down a number as quick as possible. Do not think about the question too much, as research has shown, those who answer the question immediately had better results than those who pondered over the questions too much.*

* See how to score the survey at the end.

1) I am aware of my emotions in all situations.

Always	Most of the time	Neither always/never	Almost never	Never
1	2	3	4	5

2) It is easy for me to identify my strengths.

Always	Most of the time	Neither always/never	Almost never	Never
1	2	3	4	5

3) I can easily identify my weaknesses.

Always	Most of the time	Neither always/never	Almost never	Never
1	2	3	4	5

4) When I am dealing with multiple priorities and handling stressful situations in the workplace environment, it is easy for me to manage my emotions.

Always	Most of the time	Neither always/never	Almost never	Never
1	2	3	4	5

5) I am able to handle my emotions at work during less stressful situations.

Always	Most of the time	Neither always/never	Almost never	Never
1	2	3	4	5

6) When I manage a meeting, I tend to dominate the discussion.

Always	Most of the time	Neither always/never	Almost never	Never
1	2	3	4	5

7) When I work with my staff, I often observe them interacting with others.

Always	Most of the time	Neither always/never	Almost never	Never
1	2	3	4	5

8) I am able to sense what others are feeling when I talk to them.

Always	Most of the time	Neither always/never	Almost never	Never
1	2	3	4	5

9) When I interact with team members at work, I try to interpret their emotions.

Always	Most of the time	Neither always/never	Almost never	Never
1	2	3	4	5

10) In social situations, I am usually aware of how I impact others.

Always	Most of the time	Neither always/never	Almost never	Never
1	2	3	4	5

11) I am able to understand other people's motivations by observing their behaviors.

Always	Most of the time	Neither always/never	Almost never	Never
1	2	3	4	5

12) I strive to influence the people I supervise.

Always	Most of the time	Neither always/never	Almost never	Never
1	2	3	4	5

13) I strive to influence the people I work with or on my team.

Always	Most of the time	Neither always/never	Almost never	Never
1	2	3	4	5

14) I aim to inspire others in my daily interactions.

Always	Most of the time	Neither always/never	Almost never	Never
1	2	3	4	5

15) It is important for me to work on the professional developmental needs of others.

Always	Most of the time	Neither always/never	Almost never	Never
1	2	3	4	5

16) It is important for me to develop the potential strengths in my staff.

Always	Most of the time	Neither always/never	Almost never	Never

1	2	3	4	5

Scoring:

Count how many 5's you have, how many 4's, 3's, etc. The more 1's you have, the more emotionally intelligent you may be. The more 5's you have, the less emotionally intelligence you may be. Also, do not worry about the dynamics of this scoring area. The questions you scored lowest in are those areas you need to work on to improve your score numbers. Your journey to emotional intelligence is a work in progress, and EI can improve with time, just like any other skill.

Team Cohesion Survey

This survey has been compiled from a team of researchers who investigated what makes a team a cohesive one. The survey has been used in a Master's thesis, and has produced results in finding out the cohesive nature of a team.[§]

Instructions: Take out a piece of paper, and write down numbers 1 to 13. Answer each question as you read it; write down a number as quick as possible. Do not think about the question too much, as research has shown, those who answer the question immediately had better results than those who pondered over the questions too much.*

See the scoring method at the end of the survey.

1. To which team do I belong?
Examples: Business Operations   Customer Service   Human Resources

2. The members of my team get along well together.

Agree	Somewhat agree	Neither agree/disagree	Somewhat disagree	Disagree
1	2	3	4	5

3. If given the chance, I would choose to leave my team and join another.

Agree	Somewhat agree	Neither agree/disagree	Somewhat disagree	Disagree
1	2	3	4	5

4. The members of my team will readily defend each other from criticism by outsiders.

Agree	Somewhat agree	Neither agree/disagree	Somewhat disagree	Disagree
1	2	3	4	5

5. I feel that I am really a part of my team.

Agree	Somewhat agree	Neither agree/disagree	Somewhat disagree	Disagree

1	2	3	4	5

6. I look forward to being with the members of my team each day.

Agree	Somewhat agree	Neither agree/disagree	Somewhat disagree	Disagree
1	2	3	4	5

7. I find that I generally do not get along with the other members of my team.

Agree	Somewhat agree	Neither agree/disagree	Somewhat disagree	Disagree
1	2	3	4	5

8. I enjoy belonging to this team because I am friends with many team members.

Agree	Somewhat agree	Neither agree/disagree	Somewhat disagree	Disagree
1	2	3	4	5

9. The team which I belong to is close; we are there for each other professionally and personally.

Agree	Somewhat agree	Neither agree/disagree	Somewhat disagree	Disagree
1	2	3	4	5

10. People understand their assignments in my team.

Agree	Somewhat agree	Neither agree/disagree	Somewhat disagree	Disagree
1	2	3	4	5

11. People in my team understand ways their roles contribute to the work on the whole.

Agree	Somewhat agree	Neither agree/disagree	Somewhat disagree	Disagree
1	2	3	4	5

12. My team leader is helpful to me.

Agree	Somewhat agree	Neither agree/disagree	Somewhat disagree	Disagree
1	2	3	4	5

12. My team leader supports me and encourages me in my professional growth.

Agree	Somewhat agree	Neither agree/disagree	Somewhat disagree	Disagree
1	2	3	4	5

Scoring of Team Cohesion Survey:

Look at each question number, and notice how many agree,

disagree, etc. Count up the number of each category. The more "agree" answers you have, the more cohesive your team is; the more "disagree" answers you find, the less cohesive your team is. The more neutral answers you have, the more work you have to do in identifying what needs to happen in order for the team to be cohesive. (Mixed results would also fall in this category, where you would have a mixture of agree, disagree and neutral which seem to balance out the scoring.)

§ Survey compiled from a group of researchers and items were taken from the following: Libo (1954), Beehr (1976), Seashore, Lawler, Mirvis, and Cammann (1982), Festinger (1950), Zaccaro and McCoy (1985), Feyerherm and Rice (2002).

1. Service, R. W., and Fekula, M. J. (2007). Beyond Emotional Intelligence: The EQ Matrix as a leadership imperative. *The Business Renaissance Quarterly*, 23-57, p. 24.

2. *Op. cit.* p. 28

3. *Ibid.*

4. *Ibid.*

5. Rosete, D., and Ciarrochi, J. (2005). Emotional Intelligence and its relationship to workplace performance outcomes of leadership effectiveness. *Leadership and Organizational Development Journal*, 388-399, 2005, p. 390.

6. Killburg, R. (2000). *Executive Coaching: Developing managerial wisdom in a world of chaos*. Washington, DC: American Psychological Association.

7. Blattner, J., and Bacigalupo, A. (2007). Using Emotional Intelligence to develop executive leadership and team and organizatonal development. Consulting Psychology Journal: Practice and Research, 209-219, 2007, p. 210.

8. Sosik, J., and Megerian, L. (1999). Understanding leader emotional intelligence and performance: The role of self-other agreements on transformational leadership perceptions. Group and Organizational Management, 340-366, p. 368.

9. Prati, L. M., Douglas, C., Ferris, G. R., Ammeter, A. P., and Buckley, M. R. (2003). Emotional Intelligence, Leadership Effectiveness, and Team Outcomes. *International Journal of Organizational Analysis*, 21-40, 2003, p. 28.

10. George, J. (2000). Emotions and Leadership. The role of emotional intelligence. *Human Relations*, 1027-1044, p. 1032.

11. Quincentennial Publishing Company's editor-in-chief, Gerard Mayers, wishes to thank his friend, James Lamason of Middlesex, N.J., for providing this historic and compelling example of effective team development from the period of the American Civil War.

12. Riggio, R., and Pirozzolo, F. (2002). Multiple intelligences and leadership: Implications for leadership. In R. Riggio, S. Murphy, and F. Pirozzolo, *Multiple intelligences and leadership* (pp. 241-250). Mahwah: Lawrence Erlbaum Associates.

13. Bushe, G. R., and Coetzer, G. H. (2007). Group Development and Team Effectivenss. *The Journal of Applied Behavioral Science*, 184-212, p. 188.

14. *Op. cit.*, p, 188

15. George, J. (2000). Emotions and Leadership. The role of emotional intelligence. *Human Relations*, 1027-1044.

16. White, D. W., and Lean, E. (2007). The Impact of Perceived Leader Integrity on Subordinates in a Work Team Environment. *Journal of Business Ethics*, 765-778, p. 766.

17. Robbins, S. (1994). *Essentials of organizational behavior*. Englewood Cliffs: Prentice-Hall, p. 118.

18. Feyerherm, A. E., and Rice, C. (2002). Emotional Intelligence and team performance: The good, the bad and the ugly. *The International Journal of Organizational Analysis*, 343-362, p. 348.

19. Thamhain, H. (2004). Linkages of Project Environment to Performance: Lessons for Team Leadership. *International Journal of Project Management*, 533-544, p. 536.

20. Kloppenborg, T., and Petrick, J. (1999). Leadership in Project Life Cycle and Team Character Development. *Project Management Journal*, 8-13, p. 10).

21. Rapisarda, B. A. (2002). The impact of emotional intelligence on work team cohesiveness and performance. *The International Journal of Organizational Analysis*, 363-379, p 366.

22. Shaw, M. (1976). *Group Dynamics: The Psychology of Small Group Behavior*. New York: McGraw-Hill.

23. Feyerherm, A. E., and Rice, C., *Op. cit.*, p. 359.

24. White, D. W., and Lean, E. (2007). The Impact of Perceived Leader Integrity on Subordinates in a Work Team Environment. *Journal of Business Ethics*, 765-778, p. 768.

25. Schoo, A. (2008). Leaders and Their Teams: Learning to Improve Performance with Emotional Intelligence and Using Choice Theory. *International Journal of Reality Therapy*, 40-45, p. 42.

26. Dionne, S. D., Yammarino, F. J., Atwater, L., and Spangler, W. D. (2004). Transformational Leadership and Team Performance. *Journal of Organizational Change Management*, 177-193, p. 181.

27. Bass, B., and Avolio, B. (1994). *Improving Organizational Effectiveness through Transformational Leadership*. Thousand Oaks: Sage.

28. Frye, C. M., Bennett, R., and Caldwell, S. (2005). Team Emotional Intelligence and Team Interpersonal Process Effectiveness. *Mid-American Journal of Business*, 49-56, p. 49.

29. George, *Op. cit.*, p. 1043.

30. *Ibid.*, p. 1042.

31. Conger, J. A., and Kanungo, R. N. (1998). *Charismatic Leadership in Organizations*. Thousand Oaks: Sage.

32. Goleman, D. (1995). *Emotional Intelligence: Why it can Matter More than IQ*. New York: Bantam Books.

33. Blattner, J., and Bacigalupo, A., *Op. cit.*, p. 210.

34. Prati, Douglas, Ferris, Ammeter, and Buckley, *Op. cit.*, p. 31.

35. George, *Op. cit.*.

36. Schutte, N. S., Malouff, J. M., Bobik, C., Coston, T. D., Greeson, C., Jedlicka, C., et al. (2001). Emotional Intelligence and Interpersonal Relations. *The Journal of Social Psychology*, 523-536, p. 524.

37. Sanders, K., and Schyns, B. (2006). Leadership and Solidarity Behavior: Consensus in Perception of Employees within Teams. *Personnel Review*, 538-556, p. 541.

38. Kerr, R., Garvin, J., Heaton, N., and Boyle, E. (2006). Emotional Intelligence and Leadership Effectiveness. *Leadership and Organizational Development Journal*, 265-279, p. 268.

39. Mayer, J. D., Caruso, D. R., and Salovey, P. (2000). Selecting a Measure of Emotional Intelligence: The Case for Ability Scales. In R. Bar-On, and J. Parker, *The Handbook of Emotional Intelligence: Theory, Development, Assessment, and Application at Home, School and in the Workplace*. New York: Jossey-Bass/Wiley.

40. Koman, E. S., and Wolff, S. B. (2007). Emotional Intelligence Competencies in the team and team leader. *Journal of Management Development* , 55-75, p. 58.

41. Rafaeli, A., and Worline, M. (2001). Individual Emotion in Work Organizations. *Social Science Information*, 95-123, p. 101.

42. Salovey, P., and Mayer, J. D. (1990). Emotional Intelligence. *Imagination, Cognition and Personality*, 185-211, p. 186.

43. George, *Op. cit.*, p. 1032.

44. Prati, Douglas, Ferris, Ammeter, and Buckley, 2003, p. 28.

45. Riggio, R., and Pirozzolo, F. (2002). Multiple intelligences and leadership: Implications for leadership. In R. Riggio, S. Murphy, and F. Pirozzolo, *Multiple intelligences and leadership* (pp. 241-250). Mahwah: Lawrence Erlbaum Associates.

Sources

Bass, B., and Avolio, B. (1994). *Improving Organizational Effectiveness through Transformational Leadership.* Thousand Oaks: Sage.

Blattner, J., and Bacigalupo, A. (2007). Using Emotional Intelligence to develop executive leadership and team and organizatonal development. *Consulting Psychology Journal: Practice and Research*, 209-219.

Bushe, G. R., and Coetzer, G. H. (2007). Group Development and Team Effectiveness. *The Journal of Applied Behavioral Science*, 184-212.

Conger, J. A., and Kanungo, R. N. (1998). *Charismatic Leadership in Organizations.* Thousand Oaks: Sage.

Dionne, S. D., Yammarino, F. J., Atwater, L., and Spangler, W. D. (2004). Transformational Leadership and Team Performance. *Journal of Organizational Change Management*, 177-193.

Feyerherm, A. E., and Rice, C. (2002). Emotional Intelligence and team performance: The good, the bad and the ugly. *The International Journal of Organizational Analysis*, 343-362.

Frye, C. M., Bennett, R., and Caldwell, S. (2005). Team Emotional Intelligence and Team Interpersonal Process Effectiveness. *Mid-American Journal of Business*, 49-56.

George, J. (2000). Emotions and Leadership. The role of emotional intelligence. *Human Relations*, 1027-1044.

Goleman, D. (1995). *Emotional Intelligence: Why it can Matter More than IQ.* New York: Bantam Books.

Goleman, D. (1998). *Working with emotional intelligence.* New York: Bantam Books.

Kerr, R., Garvin, J., Heaton, N., and Boyle, E. (2006). Emotional Intelligence and Leadership Effectiveness. *Leadership and Organizational Development Journal*, 265-279.

Killburg, R. (2000). *Executive Coaching: Developing managerial wisdom in a world of chaos.* Washington, DC: American Psychological Association.

Kloppenborg, T., and Petrick, J. (1999). Leadership in Project Life Cycle and Team Character Development. *Project Management Journal*, 8-13.

Koman, E. S., and Wolff, S. B. (2007). Emotional Intelligence Competencies in the team and team leader. *Journal of Management Development*, 55-75.

Kunnanatt, J. T. (2004). Emotional Intelligence: The New Science of Interpersonal Effectiveness. *Human Resource Development Quarterly*, 489-495.

Mayer, J. D., Caruso, D. R., and Salovey, P. (2000). Selecting a Measure of Emotional Intelligence: The Case for Ability Scales. In R. Bar-On, and J. .. Parker, *The Handbook of Emotional Intelligence: Theory, Development, Assessment, and Application at Home, School and in the Workplace.* New York: Jossey-Bass/Wiley.

Mayer, J. D., Salovey, P., and Caruso, D. (1999). Emotional Intelligence meets traditional standards for an intelligence. *Intelligence*, 267-298.

Mayer, J., Salovey, P., and Caruso, D. (2004). Emotional Intelligence: Theory, Findings, and Implications. *Psychological Inquiry*, 197-215.

Prati, L. M., Douglas, C., Ferris, G. R., Ammeter, A. P., and Buckley, M. R. (2003). Emotional Intelligence, Leadership Effectiveness, and Team Outcomes. *International Journal of Organizational Analysis*, 21-40.

Rafaeli, A., and Worline, M. (2001). Individual Emotion in Work Organizations. *Social Science Information*, 95-123.

Rapisarda, B. A. (2002). The impact of emotional intelligence on work team cohesiveness and performance. *The International Journal of Organizational Analysis*, 363-379.

Riggio, R., and Pirozzolo, F. (2002). Multiple intelligences and leadership: Implications for leadership. In R. Riggio, S. Murphy, and F. Pirozzolo, *Multiple intelligences and leadership* (pp. 241-250). Mahwah: Lawrence Erlbaum Associates.

Robbins, S. (1994). *Essentials of organizational behavior.* Englewood Cliffs: Prentice-Hall.

Rooy, D. L., and Viswesveran, C. (2004). Emotional Intelligence: A Meta-analytic Investigation of Predictive Validity and Nonmologicalnet. *Journal of Vocational Behavior*, 71-95.

Rosete, D., and Ciarrochi, J. (2005). Emotional Intelligence and its relationship to workplace performance outcomes of leadership effectiveness. *Leadership and Organizational Development Journal*, 388-399.

Salovey, P., and Mayer, J. D. (1990). Emotional Intelligence. *Imagination, Cognition and Personality*, 185-211.

Salovey, P., Mayer, J. D., and Caruso, D. (2002). The positive psychology of emotional intelligence. In C. Synder, and S. Lopes, *Handbook of positive psychology* (pp. 159-171). Oxford: Oxford University Press.

Sanders, K., and Schyns, B. (2006). Leadership and Solidarity Behavior: Consensus in Perception of Employees within Teams. *Personnel Review*, 538-556.

Schoo, A. (2008). Leaders and Their Teams: Learning to Improve Performance with Emotional Intelligence and Using Choice Theory. *International Journal of Reality Therapy*, 40-45.

Schutte, N. S., Malouff, J. M., Bobik, C., Coston, T. D., Greeson, C., Jedlicka, C., et al. (2001). Emotional Intelligence and Interpersonal Relations. *The Journal of Social Psychology*, 523-536.

Service, R. W., and Fekula, M. J. (2007). Beyond Emotional Intelligence: The EQ Matrix as a leadership imperative. *The Business Renaissance Quarterly*, 23-57.

Shaw, M. (1976). *Group Dynamics: The Psychology of Small Group Behavior*. New York: McGraw-Hill.

Sosik, J., and Megerian, L. (1999). Understanding leader emotional intelligence and performance: The role of self-other agreements on transformational leadership perceptions. *Group and Organizational Management*, 340-366.

Thamhain, H. (2004). Linkages of Project Environment to Performance: Lessons for Team Leadership. *International Journal of Project Management*, 533-544.

White, D. W., and Lean, E. (2007). The Impact of Perceived Leader Integrity on Subordinates in a Work Team Environment. *Journal of Business Ethics*, 765-778.

Zeidner, M., Matthews, G., and Roberts, R. D. (2004). Emotional Intelligence in the Workplace: A Critical Review. *International Association for Applied Psychology*, 371-399.

About the Author

John Errigo, MS, is a doctoral student studying organizational management and leadership. He likes to take academic and technical writings and condense them into lean publications on a variety of business topics. He is the founder of Green Oak Press, LLC and loves to research, write, and teach. He is an instructor at Chestnut Hill College, Philadelphia, Pa. John has a Bachelor of Arts from the University of Scranton in communication, a Master of Science degree from Saint Joseph's University in organizational development and training, and will have his PhD in organization management and leadership in 2013 from Capella University. He likes to connect with his readers and can be contacted through his personal e-mail of John@johnerrigo.com. He lives in Langhorne, Pennsylvania.

About the Editor

Gerard (Gerry) E. Mayers is a graduate of St. John's University in New York, New York, where he earned a Bachelor of Arts, with Honors, degree in a dual major of English and History. He brings many years of publishing and marketing experience to his position as Marketing Director for Holistic Organizational Development and Training, Inc. (HODT Inc.) and as Director of Publishing and Editor in Chief for its publishing division, Quincentennial Publishing Company (QPC). His weekly blogs on PR matters can be found on FlackMe.com, where he discusses items relevant to publc relations. In his spare time, he enjoys reading, camping, Civil War history, and volunteer work with the Boy Scouts of America. He is an award-winning program chairman for the Bucks County Civil War Roundtable. He lives with his wife, three dogs, and a cat in Milford, New Jersey.

www.ingramcontent.com/pod-product-compliance
Lightning Source LLC
Chambersburg PA
CBHW051334220526
45468CB00004B/1638

* 9 7 8 1 9 4 0 9 2 7 1 4 5 *